Schnoodle Dogs as Pets

A Complete Schnoodle Dog
Pet Owner's Guide

Schnoodle Dogs General Info, Purchasing, Care, Cost, Diet, Health, Supplies, Grooming, Training and More Included!

By: Lolly Brown

Foreword

Smart, energetic, and a down – right darling, the schnoodle has become one of the most beloved hybrid dog breeds. A Schnoodle is a cross breed of the Schnauzer and a Poodle. It comes in various colors and sizes that ranges between six and seventy – six pounds. The schnoodle is known as a lap dog, therapy dog, show dog, and of course a family dog. Most keepers described the schnoodles as a very cheerful dog, and that's probably something that the breed has inherited from the fun and people pleasing characteristics of poodles combined with the hyper active energy of the schnauzer. You can expect this dog as someone who likes to have fun, constantly interact with people, and just a really adorable pet that's the center of everyone's attention.

If you think the schnoodle resonates with you or your personality, or you want a happy dog to keep you and your family company, then this book is dedicated to you! Inside these pages, you will learn not just the history and origin of this dog breed but you'll also get to learn the nuts and bolts on how you can become the best schnoodle keeper ever! Read on about the schnoodle's history, biological information, training and grooming needs, health, and the proper diet to keep your pet healthy and happy! Have fun!

Table of Contents

Introduction

The schnoodle came about around the 1980's because there was an increased interest among hybrid breeds especially the miniature ones like the poodle. Even if the schnoodle is not as popular compared to other poodle – based hybrid dogs, it garnered enough following after its introduction – thanks to its low – shedding hypoallergenic coat, and fun playful nature. Some breeders say that the first schnoodle breed started out in Great Britain, and they're commonly known as "truffle dogs" because they know where to spot truffles on the ground.

Designer breeds like the schnoodle are first generation hybrid dogs which can lead to a genetic variety among the hybrid breeds. As mentioned earlier, the schnoodle was parented by two separate breeds – the Poodle, and the Schnauzer which is why the descriptions about this breed are mostly generalizations of the two parent dogs.

One of the reasons why people (especially those who are newbie dog keepers) choose to acquire a schnoodle is because of their adorable and fun – filled personality. Schnoodles in general are a curious and clever bunch that likes to snoop around its environment. They are very active pets that have a strong need to burn off its energy which is why it's a perfect companion for those who also have young kids. Due to their activeness and intelligence, they can easily be trained, and alson included in performance shows. They are very friendly pets, and they love to hang out with people. They can also get along with other household pets provided that there's proper introduction. As a keeper, you need to keep in mind that schnoodles really like it if you always pay attention to them, otherwise they'll try their very best to please you and make you interact with them, take it from us, these dogs doesn't run out of energy!

Unfortunately, dog breed organizations like the American Kennel Club (AKC), UKC, and CKC do not recognize hybrid designer dog breeds like a schnoodle. However, there's also lots of local kennel clubs that accept designer breeds and mixed breed dogs where keepers register their dogs for various performance shows that showcases the schnoodle's obedience, and agility. Unfortunately, due to the popularity of this designer crossbreed, several puppy mills doing improper husbandry practices have increased which is why we advise that you only buy from reputable breeders or better yet consider adopting one from rescue centers so that you can save lives and also take part in dissolving illegal puppy mill productions.

In most cases, schnoodles are bred for mini Schnauzers as well as toy and mini poodles. In fact, there's another version of schnoodles that's a crossbreed of giant Schnauzer and a standard poodle which is known as a Giant Schnoodle. Another great quality of the schnoodle that is mostly from the standard poodle dog breed is its hypoallergenic coat which is why it's best for people with allergy conditions, and they are also low – shedders making their coat easy to maintain.

Schnoodles are great companions, and a good watch dog. It's also commonly known as "Schnopoo" in the U.S. It's a devoted and loving pet that will surely bring joy to you and your family. In the next chapter, you'll learn more about these wonderful bundles of joy including its biological information, brief origin and history, quick facts, dog names, and also the pros and cons of owning one to see if this is the right dog breed for you

Chapter One: Basic Biological Information

Popularly known in the U.S. as "Schnopoo,"the schnoodle is a medium sized crossbreed designer dog. It is a mixture of a standard mini Schnauzer and a hypoallergenic poodle, and its scientific name is Canis lupus familiaris. Unfortunately, because it's a hybrid dog breed, major kennel clubs and organizations like the American Kennel Club don't recognize yet the breed but these dogs can be registered for various performance shows and agility test dog shows. It is however recognized by various hybrid dog organizations including the Designer Dogs Kennel Club (DDKC), and also the American Canine Hybrid Club (ACHC). In this chapter, we will provide you with the basic biological information about the Schnoodle breed and also their general characteristics and requirements to help you get started in knowing them and their needs.

Origin and History

It originated in the United States and was introduce to the public around the 1900's. The parent breeds of the schnoodle is the Mini Schanuzer (also known as the "Little Beard") and the Poodle (also known in Germany in "Caniche"). The Mini Schnauzer came from Germany and was used to hunt ratters in the 1800's, while the Poodle in Germany was used as a water dog to retrieve ducks around the 1500's. Dog breeders in the United States aimed to combine the intelligence and hypoallergenic coat characteristics of the Poodle with the robust and alert attitude of the Schnauzer to come up with the Schnoodle which is one of the most successful crossbreed among the designer dog breeds. The schnoodle's other nicknames include "Schnauzerdoodle,"and "Schnauzerpoo."

What owners really like about the schnoodle is its playful, interactive, and fun characteristic. It's also one of those dogs that can easily adapt to different kinds of people and can also get along with other dog breeds provided that there's proper introduction. And because of their small body structure that they've inherited from their parents breed, schnoodles are quite easy to maintain, and it doesn't need too much space which is why they are also suitable for owners living in apartments or studio type condominiums. It can happily live in a small space, and these dogs are also very friendly around young children. They are friendly and sociable but can also get a bit wary of strangers.

Facts about Schnoodles

The male schnoodle has a height of 25 to 38 cm (9.8 inches to 15 inches); its female counterpart has a slightly smaller height to the shoulder. The weight of male schnoodles is around as 14 to 24 pounds (5.4 to 11 kilogram). Female schnoodles has a relatively lesser weight than its male counterparts.

The Schnoodle's coat type varies depending on their hereditary traits that they get from their parent breeds. Usually, the schnoodle coat sports either a short or long coat that can also have a variety of soft or silky loose curly coat, a tight curl, or a straight coat. Its coat also sports various colors including the following:

- Brown

- Black

- White

- Gray

- Silver

- Sable

- Apricot

- Black & White

- Black & Tan

Grooming Needs

When it comes to grooming, how often a schnoodle should be trimmed up mostly depends on the growth of their coat and the type of coat they have. If the Schnoodle inherited the coat of a mini schnauzer then it can have higher grooming needs than those who have inherited the coat of a Poodle breed. In general, the schnoodle's coat will require high maintenance so that their coat can stay healthy, silky, soft, and/or fluffy. You'll also need to bathe your pet at least twice or thrice a month, and ensure that you regularly check their eyes, ears, nails, and teeth.

Exercise Needs

When it comes to exercise, the amount of exercise a schnoodle need depends on their size. If the dog is relatively larger than the average schnoodle then it may need more exercise (at least around half an hour to about 1 hour a day) so that they can have an outlet for their high energy.

Diet Requirements

In terms of diet, an adult schnoodle should ideally be fed two times a day. It's wise that their diet is a combination of a premium commercial dog food and a BARF diet or a balanced homemade fresh food. Later in this book we will teach you on how to prepare a healthy meal for your dog and give you some tips on what to feed them.

Health and Breeding Information

In terms of breeding, the litter size of a schnoodle is anywhere between 3 and 5 puppies. Schoodle puppies can be acquired from reputable breeders or adoption centers/ rescues. The cost will depend on the age, pedigree, health history, coat color etc. In the next chapter we will teach you how to select the right puppy that can match your personality, and how to identify a reputable dog breeder.

When it comes to their health, the main issue for schnoodles is their genetic health factors since they are a crossbreed of two dogs. They may have inherited the common illnesses found in a mini schnauzer or a poodle, maybe even both. Resolving health issues in dogs can be quite expensive which is why getting a pet insurance, and regular trips to the vet for routine checkup is necessary in order to prevent any serious health issues.

The lifespan of schnoodle breed will also vary depending on their health status, size, age, and pedigree history. Usually though the average life span of this breed is 13 to 18 years.

Suggested Dog Names

Just so you can have an idea, the common names for a male schnoodle includes the following: Jax, Spike, Ziggy, Joey, Luke, Bo, Romeo, Sparky, Ollie, and Tyson. On the other hand, common female names include Lulu, Shelby, Daisy, Cookie, Missy, Bonnie, Sasha, Pepper, Delilah and Molly.

Pros and Cons

Pros:

Schnoodles are indoor pets

If you're a newbie keeper or someone that lives in a close space like an apartment or a condo then a schnoodle can be a good size pet for you. Size wouldn't be an issue since they are a small to medium size breed that don't need too much space to roam around. Their play pen doesn't have to be very wide or an open field compared to the exercise requirements of other larger dog breeds.

Very Friendly and Easily Trained

Just like one of their parent breeds, the Poodle, they are very smart and can easily be trained even if you're a newbie dog keeper. They easily get housebreaking rules and various tricks even at a young age. They're also very acquainted with the family, loves to play with young kids, and just overall enjoy a human company.

Schnoodles have an allergen – free coat and are also a non – shedders.

Schnoodles are perfect pets for those who have asthma because they have an allergen free coat that they got from the Poodle genes. They are also non - shedders which means that you won't have any problem when it comes to cleaning up their hair around the house. The downside though is that a non – shedding coat can easily get tangled or matted which is why you need to maintain their coat through regular grooming and maintenance.

Cons

Schnoodles are barkers

If you don't like a barker, then a schnoodle may not be a good breed to keep because these dogs are prone to excessive barking which can cause some problems around your house or neighborhood when it comes to the noise. However, they can be trained at a young age to lessen their barking.

Schnoodle is not a purebred dog

As you may now know, schnoodles are designer dog breeds which mean that it is not a purebred and is therefore not recognized by any major Kennel Clubs. Don't worry though because if you're aim is to enter dog shows or join competitions, you can still do so by registering it to the American Canine Hybrid Club, and the other designer clubs mentioned earlier. However, you cannot sell a schnoodle as a purebred.

Genetic Illnesses

Schnoodles are prone to illnesses like heart disease, von Willebrand's Disease, skin allergies, retinal atrophys, and other genetic illnesses that are common and passed on by their parent breeds.

Chapter Two: Choosing the Right Puppy

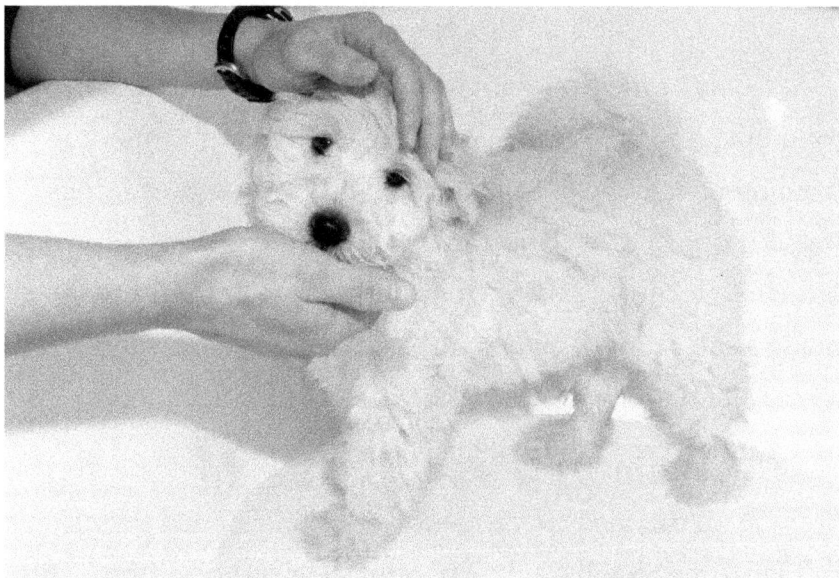

Dogs add so much to a person's life; they can be man's best friend, family companions, and also protectors but let's face it some dogs have behavioral problems. There can be various causes as to why dogs behave in certain ways. Most owners give it their best shot when it comes to training their dogs, but for some people, putting them up for adoption is the only option. Similar to people, I guess they also possess personalities which makes them unique. The good news is that you can match your own personality with your potential pet schnoodle by learning how to pick the right puppy/dog. This way you can be sure to set yourself and your dog for success, and you will both get to enjoy each other's company. This chapter will give you tips on how to find the right schnoodle pup for you!

Getting Started

One of the first things you need to do is to find a reputable dog breeder. It's best if you buy your schnoodle from breeders who specialize in breeding crossbreed dogs like this one because you can be sure that they can help you out when it comes raising your pet even after they already made a sale. What you can do is to ask your local vet for recommendations on where or who to buy a schnoodle breed from.

You can also check resources online, or ask people from forums on where they bought their puppies from. This way it can save you the time and energy in finding the right breeder. If the breeder is highly recommended by people around your area or in a particular forum, then chances are that they are responsible and reputable. However, you also need to do your own research or due diligence, and perhaps create a checklist of the qualities you like in a breeder to see if he/she fits your own criteria. It's very important that you not just make a connection with your puppy but also with the one who bred them. You can start off by asking questions to see how well they know their breeds, and also the terms of contract so that you'll be guaranteed of a quality pet.

It's also highly recommended that you consider adopting dogs from rescue centers (if in case a schnoodle is available). It will be less expensive, and you'll also get to save a life.

Steps in Picking the Right Pup

Once you've decided on where or who you're going to buy your schnoodle puppy from, it's time to find which puppy you're going to take home. You can try out the strategies or tips below when deciding which one to get especially if your breeder has quite a handful of litters.

Color Coding Technique

One of the techniques that are recommended by some dog experts is to put a ribbon on the puppies that you're going to choose from. This way you can easily identify which is which even if they look identical to one another. It'll also be easy to make mental notes to see which one you prefer.

Step 1: Observe

Once the breeder has led you to the play pen where the puppies are, all you have to do is observe how the puppies play with one another. This is where you can see if one is perhaps more active than the other, or how high/low their energy levels are. When it comes to choosing hyper dogs though, you also have to keep in mind that it may result in conflict if you are keeping another active dog at home. What you want to have is a puppy that's not shy or someone who is afraid to come to you. You can lean over them and let them sniff your finger, and see how they'll react. You don't want to pick a puppy that's intimidated or aggressive. If the puppies are interactive to you, that's a good sign of how social and friendly they are.

Step 2: Start interacting with the pups

Once you've already done step 1, you can now proceed inside the play pen and be with the puppies. This way you'll easily notice their differences, and you can also get up close to them. You may find that one might be gentler than the other, or perhaps more active than the rest. You can also ask the breeder to put in another puppy that is of a different breed (if they have any) so that you can see how the schnoodles will react and welcome another kind. This can also help you if the puppy of your choice is someone who can get along well with other dog breeds.

Step 3: Start interacting with the pups one – on – one

Once all the puppies get to know you, it's time to put them through your own "personal test" to see which one best suits you or perhaps best connect with you.

Attention Seeker

What you can do is to walk around the play pen and see which dogs follow you, and which ones aren't interested. This will help you see how much these puppies want your attention. Some puppies are jumpy, some may not be that interested in spending time with you, while some are quite social but doesn't mind to be independent. See which one best matches your preference when it comes to socialization.

Lie on the floor

The next thing you can do is to make the puppy lie on its back and see whether he/she tends to bite you or not. This will determine if the dog is someone who can easily be trained or not. Basically if the dog tries to get its teeth on you while they're lying on their backs and patting them, it can be a sign that they can be quite hard to handle and will need an owner who is a hands – on trainer perhaps. This is not necessarily a bad thing because there are some people who enjoy that, while there are some people who prefers to not make them the "chew toy." Some dogs may tend to bite, while others are fine with just you petting them.

The Cuddle Factor

You can also do what experts call as the "cuddle factor." This is where you can see if the puppy is into you, and someone whom you feel connected to. You just simply have to cuddle the puppy and hold them in your hands, and lean them over your chest or shoulder just like a baby then see how he/she will react. This may be the most fun but do keep in mind that your goal is to find the one that you can best resonate with. Some dogs might be more aggressive or playful than the others while you're cuddling them, while some could be much calmer or gentle and will enjoy a nice petting from you. A puppy who's very playful when you're holding them could be a sign that he/she needs some sort of leader to look up to, it's not a sign of dominance but perhaps they need to have some form of clarity when it comes to who they're going to obey to. Some puppy could be a quiet type wherein he/she will just enjoy cuddle times with you or lick you every now and then.

When you choose puppies from the litter, you want to look to as many puppies as you can until your objective observation is showing you that you have the right match. It's not a good idea to take one home for a 'test drive' as compared to what other people are suggesting, and that's because the dogs might become anxious if they're suddenly taken away from their home and then get returned, it may change their behavior. So make sure that when you do take one, it's for keeps.

Suppose that you get a schnoodle puppy home and you found out that he/she is doing too much chewing, what you can do is to enroll him/her to puppy obedience class/ training program. If it's a real behavior problem that doesn't mean it's a training issue, you may need help from a qualified behavioral expert.

When it comes to choosing the right schnoodle puppy, you need to have the patience to not immediately take any puppy from the first litter you've evaluated (unless of course there's only one litter from your breeder), it's wise that you check other litters before making your decision. It can be a lot of work to take a pet into your life so before buying one makes sure that you have the time, energy, and commitment in keeping a schnoodle.

Chapter Three: Housing and Crate Training Your Schnoodle

There are some keepers out there who discourage using crates for their dogs or what others call the "craters haters." These people are kind of wary when it comes to using crates or cages for their dogs because it comes across as something inhumane and cruel. Here's the thing, these people may have misunderstand how a crate is use, and perhaps they're talking about what they like rather than what their dogs prefer. You see if you think of it as a cage where you dog will get locked up then most probably that's how you're going to use it which is why some owners have this sort of misconception when it comes to using crates for their dogs.

If you happen to be one of these "crater haters" or just a newbie keeper wondering what kind of cage/ craters are out in the market, this chapter will enlighten you and give you some advice on how to crate train your schnoodle pup.

Crate for Your Schnoodle

Before we get into the different types of crates that are available in the market today, we'll first discuss the purpose and importance of why you need to buy a crate for your pet and hopefully ward you off of the misconceptions about the cage being 'inhumane' to dogs.

We, humans like the idea of having 'space' and 'freedom.' We tend to like a house with open floor plans, a huge backyard, or a property to roam around in for some reason but here's the difference between humans and animals particularly with dogs; dogs are denning creatures. Ultimately, these pets like it when it's 'dark and close.' It's the same with cats, birds, spiders, and other creatures. You also have to understand that whether you buy your pet a crate or not, your schnoodle is most probably denning up one way or another. This is the reason why dogs like to sit or hang out below coffee tables or any tables for this matter, hangout under your desk, or hide under the blankets. This is also the reason why some dogs prefer to nestle in bolster beds and sleep under cushions or why they sleep under the chairs or under your couch, and even in your closet. Sure your schnoodle will tend to play outside and enjoy the wide space around but at the end of the day, they like to den up to whatever fashion they're comfortable with in your house. Even if the schnoodle is a very sociable dog, they'd still want to have their own space or have that sense of privacy so to speak at some point, whether it's between their keepers on the bed or lounging on their bed. Whenever you will leave your pet on a place somewhere in the house, say the kitchen or in the living room, you've created a den for them.

A crate is a soft and protective den that your dog can use whenever you're not around to be with them. There are some dogs who don't need crates but those are the outliers. Majority of dogs especially puppies will surely benefit from crate training and its useful function.

Contrary to some keepers, crates should never be used to punish a dog. Never lock them up inside the crate when you're angry at them because it'll only teach them to fear the crate which can affect your pet's behavior and create problems in the long run.

Pros and Cons of Using Crates

Crates are useful especially if you're raising a puppy or aiding a new adult dog to settle in their new environment. While your pet schnoodle is learning your house rules, using a crate can help you control destructive behaviors. These are some things you need to consider:

- **Environmental Management**: It would be wise if you don't let your puppy or dog get tempted in chewing things by blocking their access to certain things around the house like shoes or clothes.

- **Errorless Housetraining for puppies**: Crates can be necessary and quiet effective when it comes to housetraining your Schnoodle puppy.

- **Crates provide housetraining for newly adopted dogs**: Crates can also be useful if ever you have adopted a matured or adult schnoodle. However, even if that's the case, they still need to do the full housetraining. For mature dogs that already have gone through the potty training process, a crate not be necessary but if ever your adult pet has a behavior problem you're trying to address then a crate can be a useful component to your treatment plan.

Even for those dogs that don't need a crate, crate training is still essential because it could build up their character as you may need your dog to go to the crate at some point nonetheless. Say for example, they need a place to stay while you're off somewhere or while waiting their turn at the groomers, they will need to spend time inside the crate. It's also a safe option whenever you plan on bringing your schnoodle while travelling as it can be a familiar and reliable place inside the car for your dog, and you're guaranteed that they won't cause any distraction while you're driving especially since schnoodles are quite active pets.

At home, it's essential to have areas of inclusion and also confinement. You need to somehow control your pet's stimulation and compartmentalize it in places you want. It's quite irresponsible if you just leave it up to chance, and using a crate will help.

Do keep in mind that a crate shouldn't be used for extended periods because it obviously doesn't provide any outlet for your schnoodle's high energy. If your dog is spending time in a crate then ensure that you counter that confinement by providing an outlet for physical exercise and mental stimulation.

A crate can be an effective management tool but it's definitely not a substitute for a 'baby – sitter.'

Types of Crates

There are various types of crates available but here's the quick rundown of the most commonly used crates among dog keepers.

Plastic Crates

These are the original standard for crates. It's also great as your schnoodle's first crate. Plastic crates are very easy to clean up because you can disassemble it so that you can do a spot – cleaning. Generally, plastic crates are warmer and drier. It's also very easy to just throw a blanket on it to create a dark and denned up space for your pet schnoodle. Plastic crates are good for cars or whenever you're travelling with your pet, some crates can also be easily strapped to the car seat. Plastic crates are also the only option whenever you're riding an airplane if ever the airline doesn't allow pets in the cabin as most plastic crates comply with airline safety standards. In addition to all of these, it's one of the most affordable crates available.

Wire Crates

The 2nd most common type of crate is a wire crate. It can easily be fold up for storage or transport. Dogs like to stay in a wire crate because it provides more circulation and vision unlike with plastic crates where they're really in a tight space. Some of the cons include it being quite clunky and heavy (depending of course on its size), it's also not allowed on planes. It's also a great use while in the car if you have enough space, and it's has lots of affordable options.

Soft – Sided Crates

It's also easily foldable like wire crates but the main difference is that it's made up of nylon, vinyl, and also aluminum or other lightweight materials. It's also best use for travels and campings. However, these are not recommended for dogs suffering from anxiety or those that are distressed. It's also not advisable for the crate training process. This is perhaps only good for dogs that have been trained already and are comfortable in using crates. It's also affordable but relatively expensive than the first two types.

Fashion Crates

These are crates made out of finer materials that are meant to look like a furniture. Some crates are also customized to look like a furniture. This type of crate is best suited for dogs who have already gotten accustomed to using crates. It comes in various shapes and sizes but fashion crates tend to be quite expensive especially if the design is superb.

Heavy Duty Crates

These are crates that are best for long transports. It's mostly used by keepers who travel with their pets on a regular or frequent basis like those dogs who are always included in competitions or performance shows. This is also the safest option when travelling in cars because it's built to withstand a full on car crash. These crates are very expensive but also worth the investment especially if you plan on joining competitions or travelling in different places.

Exercise Pens

These are also great addition for your pet schnoodle because it can be a great integration for your dog's housetraining. It's also good for small puppies and small to medium sized breeds like the schnoodle. It's also a great inclusion space when your dog transition from the crate. It's very easy to set up; it's also foldable and movable plus it's quite affordable. It's important to note though that before you toss off your pet to an exercise playpen you should also spend some time training them to just play inside because if not they can easily get out once they get big enough, and it'll be useless.

Crate Tip:

Lots of keepers and professional trainers highly recommend that you buy both a wire crate and a plastic crate. Of course, it'll be use at different occasions. The wire crate will function as an inclusion crate wherein the dog is housed but it's still in close proximity with its owners. On the other hand, the plastic crate will function as the quiet crate which will provide your pet with some quiet time alone. Once you've crate trained your dog, you can eventually progress in housing them in the other types of crates, and they'll have no problem adjusting to it hence it will serve as their safe space.

Size of the Crate

The most common suggestion of keepers when it comes to the size of the cage is that the crate should be big enough for the dog to stand up, turn around, and lie down. This suggestion may be useful if you're adopting a more mature schnoodle but for puppies it might be quite difficult. Wire crates usually come with a small divider so that once your pet starts growing, you can easily adjust and enlarge the cage so that you don't need to keep buying. However, for your plastic crate you may need to buy a crate big enough to accommodate your schnoodle's growth.

Crate Training

Habituation

If ever your pet had a previous bad experience when it comes to being housed in crates or he/she is suffering from separation anxiety/ isolation distress, then you may need to ask help from a professional dog trainer or behavioral consultant. Never force your pet to live in it if they don't feel comfortable inside because it may worsen their distress in the long run. Keep in mind that your goal here is to let your dog view the crate as a safe place that's also a pleasant and comfortable environment.

This is why habituating them is important; you're aiming to have a good conditional emotional response for your schnoodle.

Timing

As with any other dog training, timing is everything. You need to be able to monitor your pet's energy. Never try to crate train them during their 'peak arousal' times or a period within the day where you think they are most active. Ideally, you want to crate train them once they've already worn out or tired after playing around all day because that will initiate them to settle down inside their crate and take some rest after a long day.

Tips in Crate Training Your Pet

Tip #1: Use your voice and praise your dog. Keep in mind that your voice is first and foremost your training tool. You need to also consider using a consistent phrase to cue your pet to go inside its crate. Pairing a word/ phrase will help when you're instructing your pet and catching their attention towards where it needs to be.

Tip #2: Tie the back door of the crate. You should initially use a lock or something so that the door wouldn't swing back and forth so that it wouldn't scare your schnoodle.

Tip #3: Keep a bowl of treats and some toys in the crate. Keeping a bowl of treats when you're doing crate training will be handy because it will function as pre – bait for your dog. Chew toys is also essential because you'll need to reward it afterwards. Never crate train your dog if you don't have food and toy rewards. You must set it up beforehand so that it can be convenient for you once you start training your pet.

Tip #4: Avoid predictable crate training times. Routines are great but make sure that your training follow – up is not predictable for your pet. What you need to do is to destabilize any pattern that will short – circuit your dog's expectation. This way it will help preserve the integrity of your crate training.

Tip #5: Never let your dog make a habit of demanding to be let up in the crate. As you may now know, crate training is quite labor intensive but it lessens the onset of many problems in the long run. You need to be patient and continue practicing your pet to go to the crate willingly. It may probably take several days to a few weeks or maybe even longer so don't rush it. Observe your dog as it will have its own pace of learning.

Using the Crate

Duration

When it comes to duration, you can practice to leave your dog inside the crate for just about 30 minutes while you leave the house. After that, you can try leaving them inside for an hour. Keep in mind that you shouldn't create a grand exit when you're about to leave them inside their crate because if you do, they might come out too hot or launch out like an aggressive dog once you let them out of the cage. Your pet may also become reluctant to go inside again. Be a bit enthusiastic about getting your pet inside the crate, and kind of neutral when letting them out.

Provide a bed crate

You can provide a pad or mat inside the crate or a towel especially if your dog is chewing the bed at least until the chew training is done.

Puppy Bladder

Puppies that are being potty trained should not be put inside the crate longer than they are expected to hold their pees/poos. The rule of thumb is to let them stay for around 1 hour if the puppy is still a month old. It will then progress to 2 to 3 hours once they are 2 months old; 3 to 4 hours once they reach 3 months, and so on. Until the potty training is completed, ensure that you're around at lunch break or if not ask your friend or helper to let the puppy out of its crate after a few hours to supervise your dog.

For adult dogs, they won't need as much potty breaks compared to puppies. However, those dogs who are just newly adopted should still get potty trained as well as crate training.

Food and Water

Never leave food inside the crate when you're not around. This is because you don't want to free - fed your schnoodle. It is best that you set up a routine timed feeding. You shouldn't also let your dog stay inside the crate for so long where it'll require them to have food available. Perhaps the only time that you need to provide food inside its crate is when you're chew training them in order to teach them a habit of using the crate but of course it's only a temporary reward during your dog's training.

When it comes to providing water, if you're only going to leave your dog inside its crate for a while then water isn't necessary but if you need to leave your pet behind for several hours while you go off to work, you should consider making water available. If that's the situation, then make sure that you use a water bottle instead of a bowl because it's a lot less messy since your dog can trip on their bowls or even contaminate it.

If ever you need to leave your dog behind every day alone then you may want to consider creating a 'dog apartment' so that they can have a larger space to hang out, and even provide a toilet where your puppies can relieve themselves. You can check out dog online websites to gather ideas on how you can set up a dog apartment.

Importance of Using Inclusion Crate and Quiet Crate

As previously mentioned, a wire crate functions as an inclusion crate, and a plastic crate is more of a quiet crate for your schnoodle, both of these crates are useful for managing your schnoodle's high energy around the house. There will be times where your dog needs to settle down and den themselves up, and there'll also be times where they need to spend time with you/ your family but still needs to learn their own 'space,' since you're there to supervise them, it's the best time to chew train your dog using chew toys, and also teach them how to use the exercise pen. Whatever kind of crate set up you do for your pet, make sure that it's located somewhere you can adjust easily, and where you can monitor them. Don't put it in the far corner of the house or upstairs. Make it easy and convenient for both you and your pet schnoodle.

Chapter Four: Supplies for Your Schnoodle

After buying a crate, it's now time to learn all the other supplies you need to buy for your new pet! You'll learn in this chapter the various accessories that will be helpful for your pet when they're around the house just hanging out with your or whenever you're training them/ walking them. The accessories and basic necessities included here will take a cut off of your monthly budget but that's what you need to do as a responsible keeper. Just consider it a great investment because it'll make your pet happy, healthy, and he'll also get to enjoy your company.

Food and Water

First off is food and water. Obviously this is the most important requirement not just for dogs but for all household pets. You can provide tap water for your pet schnoodle if it's potable; you can also give them bottled water especially if they're still a puppy or whatever you prefer as long as it's fresh and clean.

When it comes to providing dog food, you can easily have lots of options based on your preferred brand, nutrients included or ingredients you'd like for your dog, their age and other considerations. You can provide them with commercial kibble foods, wet food, BARF diets etc. If you want to ensure that you're feeding the right nutrition for your pet schnoodle regardless of their age or health condition, it's best that you consult your dog's vet so that they can give you ideas on what kind of diet your schnoodle needs. You can also go online and do your own research, or you can also ask other schnoodle keepers on how to go about when it comes to feeding them.

Your goal of course is to try and get the best nutrition to feed your schnoodle but also something that's affordable and within your monthly budget.

When it comes to the feeding amount, there are lots of factors you need to consider including your dog's age and weight, their preference, related health condition etc. It's going to boil down to what works for your pet as long as it will make them healthy, happy, and is something approved by your vet, that's all you need to know.

Bowls

You'll need to get food/ water bowls because that's where you're dog is going to eat its food. As we've mentioned earlier, you can also buy a water dripper so that you lessen the risk of your dog spilling the water in the bowl or even contaminating it especially if you're not around.

One of the main things you need to consider is the size. Obviously, if your dog is big then you need to provide a larger bowl, and if they are small to medium size like the schnoodle then a relatively smaller size will do. You also need to consider the material that the food/ water bowls is made out of. The available options out there are plastic, metal, and ceramic bowls; it's up to you on which do you prefer but many keepers suggest that you use a metal or ceramic type because it doesn't harbor bacteria unlike the plastic bowl.

It's also much easier to clean and very durable. Other types of bowls you might encounter include slow feeding bowls; this kind is best for dogs who like to chomp down their food easily, you may want to buy this one if you think your schnoodle is eating quickly all the time because that's not good for their digestion. The slow feeders may be a bit expensive but just consider it as an investment because it'll be good for your schnoodle's health in the long run.

Do keep in mind that you need to regularly spot clean your pet's food and water bowls since your dog isn't just eating there but also licking the whole bowl. You don't want to harbor bacteria in there so better clean it up nicely every day to avoid any onset of illness. You can also buy a few extras if you like so that you have a new bowl ready. Another thing to remember is to ensure that you're only giving them the right amount that they need or the amount of food that they can consume to avoid any leftovers as it can also gather up bacteria if it's not replaced.

Dog Bed

Even if your pet schnoodle is a highly active dog, they will at some point need a place to rest which is why providing them a bed is important. Again, you need to consider various factors when choosing the kind of bed for your schnoodle including their current size, material, and the season. You need to consider the environment that you live in because it'll obviously affect the temperature in the house. If you live in a hotter climate, you can just buy a simple soft cotton rug and place it somewhere in your house where your pet can lay, or place it inside the crate; this way your dog will find it relaxing despite of the hot weather. If you live somewhere cold or during the winter season, you may need to buy another bed that's cozier, thick, snuggly, and a bed that could make your dog warm during the cold days.

Just like with food bowls, cleaning your pet's bed on a regular basis is very important. You need to consider how you're going to easily clean it, say you just want something that you can easily put on the washing machine or can be easily washed by hand if that's what you prefer. Make sure though that you'll use dog friendly products, and something that's not going to damage the bed's material.

Collar and ID

Dog collars are one of the most important things you need to buy for your pet because it doesn't only function as something that can control your dog if you're out walking, it's also helpful because if ever your dog gets out of the house without you knowing it will less likely be picked up by the pound, and if your schnoodle has a name tag on it with your phone number, then people can bring it back to you as soon as possible if ever it gets lost. You might also want to consider getting your pet micro-chipped because even if the dog ID can help your dog can lose the name tag or its collar. If its micro – chipped then the schnoodle can still be identified by people and be returned to you.

Lead

Some dogs like the schnoodle will need to be out for a walk at least every other day which is why buying a lead can also come in handy so you can easily attached it to the collar and walk them. It's not just great for walking as it can also be used when you're implanting a certain behavior in them at home or whenever you're training them. It's great for keeping them under control and also during your potty training.

When you do buy a lead, make sure that it's strong enough to hold your dog, and the handle should also be comfortable for you so that when your schnoodle pulls away you don't injure your hand. In addition to picking out the material of the lead, you also need to consider the strength of the hook at the end because that's what's going to be attached to your pet's collar/ harness because you obviously wouldn't want it to break once your pet pulls away, otherwise you'll end up losing your dog. It's wiser in the long run to spend a bit more money when purchasing a durable and comfy lead.

Brush

How often you'll brush your dog's coat will ultimately depend on the type of coat they have. If your pet is long – haired or has a thick coat then you need to brush your schnoodle many times a weekm on the other hand if they are short – haired then you most likely need to brush them just once or twice a week. The type of brush will highly depend on your pet's coat type, you can find lots of options available but make sure that it's something suitable for your pet otherwise their coat will suffer from it. You can do online research on what kind of brush is best for your pet schnoodle or you can ask fellow keepers if they have any suggestions. You can also ask your local groomer for advice on what brush to buy.

Toys

Every dog breeds need toys to play with especially a schnoodle puppy! It keeps your dog entertained especially if you're not around to play with them. It's highly recommended that you get various toys initially for your pup just so you can know what kind of toys he prefers to play with. You can buy affordable toys but something that's also of good quality, this is because if you buy an expensive one, you're not sure if your dog is going to like it or if what if they just destroy it? It'll then be a waste of money so make sure to get a couple of cheap toys at first that's also mentally and physically stimulating to them.

Some examples include balls, squeakers, and different types of chew toys. Once you've learned what kind he prefers then you can go ahead and buy a couple more of that or perhaps spend more money on the stuff that your schnoodle loves. It's also highly recommended that you buy interactive toys like a Frisbee so that he/she can play it with you. Playing with them and taking part in this activity can help you build a strong bond with your pet.

Dog Shampoo

You also need to get your pet a dog – friendly shampoo that you'll use during bathing time. You can get some from your local pet shop or online. You'll see lots of different brands so just make sure that you check the ingredients before deciding what to buy because some dogs are allergic to certain stuff. To be safe just choose a simple puppy shampoo that's gentle on a dog's skin or coat. You can also try shampoo with organic ingredients. Keep in mind though that you don't really need to always bathe your dog unless they already stink so bad or gets really dirty; you can just bathe them once or twice a month or as needed because if you bathe them too much it can damage their skin/coat and also wash away their natural oil.

Optional Items

Harness

These things are optional but many keepers use it because it provides better control when you're walking your pet. It doesn't strain them too much since it's attached to the body if ever they pull you compared to a leash that can strain their neck. Just like picking a leash or collar, you want to buy something that's comfortable for your pet's body and also durable. There are lots of options and designs but just make sure that it's the right size for your pet and it's also made out of great material preferably with pads. It's a great investment for your pet and it'll also last for a long time.

Clicker

Clickers are optional but it can be helpful especially if you're training or housebreaking your schnoodle puppy. Majority of dogs respond to clickers and can really benefit your dog in the long run.

Training Treats

This comes in handy whenever you're training your puppy because it'll serve as their reward. You can buy different kinds of training treats online or in your local pet shops, and you can even make them your own. Usually it's just a bite – size food that won't make your dog too full when it's time for their actual meal. You need to have at least a bowl of treats with you during their training, and keep in mind that it should also be low – fat but still enticing for your schnoodle so that they'll cooperate with you during training.

Deodorizer Spray

This can be helpful if you have many soft fabrics in your house as it can provide great smell in your couch, rug or other soft furniture around your home. Just make sure that you buy a dog friendly deodorizer spray.

Fur and Nail Clippers

You may need this if you choose to not take your pet to the groomer and just do it yourself. You need to invest in dog coat clippers, scissors or brush, and also safe nail clippers. You can ask your local groomer for recommendations and they could also provide you with some brands that are great for your dog's coat.

Child Gates

This is part of puppy – proofing your house and will come in handy if there's a part of the house that you don't want your schnoodle to have access to. As they get older and have completed their training then your schnoodle may not need it anymore but if they are still pups, its best that buy a child gate so that you can prevent your pet from accidentally wandering or sneaking in without your supervision.

Chapter Five: Feeding Your Schnoodle with BARF Diet

There are various types of dog foods that you can find in local pet shops, groceries, and online stores; you may also encounter breed specific dog foods. It's wise to ask your vet regarding the kind of food brands that's best to feed to your dog or the type of diet because it will vary depending on your dog's age, size, weight, and the likes.

The important thing when choosing food is that it must be made out of high quality ingredients and there shouldn't too much filler in it, if not at all. You should check the ingredients and as much as possible try to avoid 'grocery branded foods' because it's usually just filled with unhealthy stuff. Keep in mind that money spent on a quality dog food is money saved on the trip to the vet's office. This chapter will guide you on what is known as a BARF dog diet that's both made out of organic food ingredients and a balanced homemade meal.

Nutrition for Your Schnoodle

When it comes to the body structure or physique of your pet schnoodle, it doesn't matter if he looks 'thin.' They should in fact look sturdy and not fluffy or bloated. They should be active, capable of running fast, and walking without catching their breath too much. If ever youyou're your pet breathing heavily after running or walking, then it's best to consult your vet. When giving nutrition for your pet, just make sure that you never feed your pet more than the amount he/ she needs. Consult your breeder and you're your veterinarian for advice on whether your schnoodle needs more food or maybe additional supplements and vitamins, but do not feed him or her additional food just because he appears to be thin – looking.

Most keepers switch foods once their pups hit nine months. It's still best to consult your breeder or vet so you can ensure what age is appropriate to change their diet. Some people introduce adult food earlier than nine months, while some do it a little over ten months which is why it's best to ask your vet/ breeder about it as they already have knowledge and experience regarding this matter.

BARF Diet

BARF stands for Biologically Approved Raw Foods; it's one of the best types of dog diets today, and it's also better than just feeding your pet with commercial food brands. The main question of newbie keepers regarding the BARF diet is this: "Why feed raw?" Well, you really can't argue with Mother Nature because dogs have eaten natural food for thousands of years. Simply put, a natural diet such as the BARF diet doesn't contain any sort of preservatives that's usually found in commercial dog foods which can cause digestive problems or other health issues in the long run.

Some of the benefits of BARF diet include cleaner dog teeth and fresh breath, lean weight, improved digestion, healthy coat and skin, lessens the risk of food allergy, harder, and less stinky stools/ improves bowel health, more stamina, increased mobility, help maintain a high energy level, strong immune system, improves liver, and pancreatic health. On top of all this the main benefit of a healthy dog is the money you'll save due to fewer trips to the vet.

Some keepers think that these canine animals are omnivores because they eat both veggies and meat which is a fact but that's only because they would pretty much eat anything. However, by nature, dogs are carnivores. Their digestive system is naturally set to digest meat since they have strong and powerful digestive juices. Dogs in general are designed to eat flesh meat. If you study their anatomy, dogs have short intestines, have strong jaw bones, and sharp teeth that are meant to cut and rip meats. So that only means that even though they can eat other type of foods like vegetables or human scrapes, their primary diet should be carnivorous.

This is where BARF diet comes in; the main ingredients of a BARF diet are bones, raw meat, veggies, fruits, organs, and supplements.

The BARF Ingredients

The ingredients you'll need can all be found in a local supermarket. We list some of the ingredients you can try below for your pet schnoodle:

Meat:

- Raw chicken with bones (small/ bite – sized/ large; depending on the age/size of your dog)
- Frozen Minced Turkey
- Frozen Minced Chicken
- Egg (1)
- Beef chunks

Veggies/ Fruits

- Carrots (at least 1)
- Apples (1 to 2 apples sliced)
- Broccoli (just a handful of chooped broccolis)

What you can do with the ingredients listed above is to blend first the couple of veggies like the carrots, apples, and broccoli. You can go ahead and chop it up to a few pieces, mix it with a bit of water, and blend it. Then you can place the minced turkey/chicken on the food bowl as ease, and pour in the blended veggie juices. After doing that, you can just slightly mash and mix the veggies juices with the meat. You can then add the egg because it's also a great source of protein for your pet. And the last step is to add chicken with bone on top of that. Now of course, the amount you'll give should depend on your pet's current size. It's best to consult your vet with regards to how much do you need to feed your schnoodle if you'd like to provide him with a BARF diet. You can also add in dog multivitamins once or twice a day depending on what your vet tells you. Usually though, you don't really need to give vitamins to youd pet if you're giving him a BARF diet but some keepers still likes providing vitamins just so it can supplement their dog's diet.

You can also buy a ready – made mixed fruit and vegetable and add it on your minced turkey/chicken, chicken bone, and egg so that you won't have to chop up individual veggies or fruits. In addition, you can also use the egg shells because it's also a great source of calcium. Some keepers just leave out the egg shell but it's much better if you crunch it up using a mortar and pestle so that it can easily be digested by your schnoodle. Just sprinkle it on top, and give it all a nice mix.

Feeding Schedule

It's important that you follow the meal routine set by your breeder (which can be around 3 to 4 times a day). Avoid overfeeding and giving him table craps because their stomachs at this age is not yet strong enough and could most likely upset his stomach.

- **3 to 4 months:** 2 meals per day (same food)
- **7 to 9 months:** 1 meal a day
- **8 to 10 months onwards:** 1 meal a day (you can gradually start switching to adult dog foods)

The Lazy Man's BARF Diet

The easiest way to feed your dogs with BARF diet if you haven't got the time to do all that is to just buy it from the store. There are food brands that have a mixture of fruits/ veggies, and minced meat all together. It's frozen and ready to go whenever you need to feed your dog. Of course, you can still crack an egg to top it off, and provide a raw chicken with bone. Make sure that the chicken bone is raw; otherwise the bones will splinter and could get stuck in your dog's digestive track. Raw chicken bones are chewy and great for your schnoodle. Aside from raw chicken bones, you can add beef chunks on its meal. Of course, it's up to you on what other veggies/ fruits/ meat you want to add but just make sure that you've consulted your vet regarding the ingredients you're going to add to ensure that it would be healthy for your pet.

Chapter Six: House Training and Grooming Your Schnoodle

Grooming your schnoodle is very important as it can help maintain their fur or coat, and also prevent any mite infestations that could bring about allergies or skin infections. In addition to that, grooming is a great way for you to bond with your newfound friend! It'll get your schnoodle used to your touch and makes him more open to human handling especially at a young age, which is why it's best to start grooming your puppy as early as possible. This chapter will not just cover your schnoodle's grooming needs, we will also give you tips and tricks on how you can train your dog to behave well and learn the house rules so that he'll treat you as the 'leader' of the pack and be obedient to you in the long run.

House Training Your Schnoodle

House training your dog isn't really hard but it does require that you'd be consistent about it. Otherwise you're never going to succeed, or at least it the knowledge wouldn't be sustainable for you and your pet. The tips and tricks that we're going to share with you is more focused on puppies since the pet schnoodle you're going to acquire is mostly at a young age but don't worry because this is also applicable to adult/matured schnoodles.

As you now know, Schnoodles are not just active pets but they're also quite clever and eager to learn, although at times they are quite witty and a bit stubborn which is why training them while they're still a puppy will increase your chances of having a well-behaved and obedient matured dog. When it comes to dog training, there are many different methods to choose from. Below you will find an overview of each training method below:

Training Method #1: This method is known as positive reinforcement, and this kind of method hinges on your schnoodle's natural desire to please its owner. The goal of this method is to train your pet to repeat desired behaviors through giving them rewards right after they do it. For instance, if you want your dog to go inside its crate or sit, you can teach him what the command means, and once he successfully do it you can then reward your pet each time he responds to the command appropriately.

Training Method #2: The next method you can try is with the help of a dog clicker or what is known as the clicker training. The essence in positive reinforcement training lies in helping your pet to identify the desired behavior, and that is where the clicker comes in. You go through the normal process of training, giving your dog a command and guiding him to perform the desired behavior. The main difference is that as soon as your schnoodle displays the behavior, you first click the clicker so that it'll caught his attention, and become aware of what he did, then immediately give him a treat. Many keepers find this tool helpful because it let the dog become aware of the action, and also learn more quickly. However, it's important to note that you should only use the clicker during the first few repetitions of a training sequence until your schnoodle learns what the desired behavior is otherwise he'll only depend on it in the long run.

Training Method #3: This is also known as the "submission training technique." This means that you must make your pet must learn how to be submissive to you so that he'll follow your will or desired training. The submission training involves things like never letting your pet walk through the door before you, or waiting to feed your dog until after you have eaten. However, there are some keepers who are quite hesitant to use this kind of technique for various reasons. It's worth a shot though since dogs are naturally inclined to follow a leader. If you establish yourself as the leader, he/she will naturally submit to you and make the training a lot easier and perhaps long – lasting.

Grooming Your Schnoodle

We've mentioned in the previous chapters that perhaps the major downside of owning a schnoodle is the coat maintenance or the grooming part, and that's mainly because even if these dogs aren't shedders, their coats are sometimes quite hard to trim and brush especially if you decided to do it yourself, and not bring him to a local groomer. However, once you've gotten used to it and learned ways on how you can handle the curly/ thick coats of your pet, it'll be easier for you as you go along. In addition, grooming can also be the time when you give your pet a thorough check up of his body. You can check for any sort of lumps, parasites, mites, cuts and prevent skin or ear problems.

You should also keep in mind to never shave your schnoodle's coat. A dog's coat protects them from the sun, rain, and snow. If you want your pet to maintain a nice soft/silky fur, you can do that by feeding them with foods like fish that are rich with omega fatty acids. These types of food can help improve your pet's skin, make their coat glossy, and maintain their hypoallergenic characteristic.

Do – It –Yourself Grooming

Some of the basic things when it comes to grooming your schnoodle are as follows. Take note though that some brushes are useful only for specific kinds of coats, consult your groomer for advice on what to use:

- Shed blade
- Coat rake
- Rubber curry brush
- Wide – toothed metal comb
- Pin brush
- Dog – friendly shampoo and conditioner
- Towel
- Blow Dryer
- Nail Clippers

How to Bathe and Brush Your Schnoodle

Before you do anything ensure to brush off all the loose fur/coat, and make sure that there are no mats. Brush their coat a bit before soaking it with water. Otherwise, if you put your schnoodle under the water without brushing you will tangle up his hair even more.

If you're going to bathe your pet inside your bathroom or say in the bathtub, then make sure that you provide a rubber mat or a towel to prevent him from slipping off. If you're going to bathe him outside, say in your backyard, then you don't need to put a rubber mat but it can still come in handy.

Do keep in mind that dog's don't like bathing in general especially if you're residing in an area where there's really cold temperatures. Ideally, you want to bathe them once or twice a month or when it's really necessary (they got into a mud etc.). Some keepers bathe their dogs every other week or more often, it's entirely up to you and the living condition you have but just don't do it on a frequent basis.

Now, once you've prepared everything you need like the towel, rubber mat, shampoo, soap, water etc., and you have removed all the tangles in the coat then it's time to wet your dog with lukewarm water. It'll probably take around 5 to 10 minutes to wet him all over.

Once you've done that, the next step is to apply shampoo/conditioner/dog soap. However, before you do make sure that it's diluted with water. It's important to keep in mind that the shampoo/ soap you use must be dog – friendly and doesn't have strong ingredients. Never use your own shampoo as this could be harmful for your pet. You should also be careful when applying the shampoo near their eyes.

In addition, you can use a rubber curry brush and rub it to your pet to stimulate its body oils. You should opt to use a conditioner with sunscreen as well. Once that's all taken care of, and you've already given your pet a good rub all over its body, it's time to rinse him off. Make sure that there's no trace of shampoo left as it could irritate your pet and make him/ her itch. After that, dry him off using a towel and blow dryer. Dry him off and use a blow dryer to dry the water on his skin. Blow drying can also blow away the residue and loose fur in your pet's coat. Use a coat rake to brush him and entangle carefully any loose furs.

When it comes to brushing your pet's coat, you'll find that you'll rake more than just brush as some of the schnoodle's coats are quite thick. The goal of brushing though is to always get rid of the loose hair and keep the coat smooth and clean. Make sure to brush the coat of your pet at least once or twice a week. You can use a wide –

toothed comb to do regular brushing as its rounded off tip will not hurt your pet's body.

For Schnoodle's with Thick Coat

- **Get rid of the clumps of hair.** This is where you'll need the shed blade. After getting rid of the clumps of hair, you should brush your schnoodle with a coat rake or other brush that would best suit your dog's coat. You can start from the head and work towards the rest of its body.

- **Add a few drops of conditioner in the water and spray it to your dog's coat.** The conditioner will help control the loosen furs and also prevent hurting as you untangle some mats in your schnoodle's coat.

- **Use the comb to untangle the mats and knots if there's any and loosen the dead hair.** Don't pull off the mats as this will hurt your pet. Brush the coat all over its body by using a fine – toothed comb to also brush the fur under its skin, chin, tail, and ears. Take the brush and comb its coat forward over its head and shoulders. Remember to also comb out the hair in its legs and rear end

- **Finishing Touches!** Use the metal comb to comb the coat and flatten it out, then add some finishing touches by using a regular pin brush. You can also trim up some excess fur in its feet or toes to make him look neat.

Removing Fleas Off Your Dog

Household pets like dogs are quite prone in flea/ tick infestations on their coats. This is the reason why you need to groom up your pet and always do a routine check on their coat to ensure that there are no ticks, fleas or mites living in their hair. One way of doing that is to use forceps. When removing ticks or fleas, make sure you lift out the entire thing and not leave some parts of it behind. Once you spot a tick, you can dab it over with some regular Vaseline so that it wouldn't hurt as much when you pull it out. You might encounter a reddish spot where the tick was clinging but that's fine. Just make sure to wash the area or dab on some antibacterial ointment that's recommended by the vet.

Cleaning Your Schnoodle's Teeth and Gums

Keeping your dog's teeth and gums clean and free of any tartar is essential to its health because it can help improve their digestion and also prevent any internal illnesses. You can ask your vet or your breeder to show you how you can properly and carefully brush your pet's teeth. Usually when you take your dog out for a check – up, your vet will clean your dog's teeth and scrape off the tartar. If ever you're going to follow the BARF diet we mentioned in the previous chapter, it'll make your dog's teeth healthier. A healthy gums and teeth will enable your schnoodle to properly eat their food which can help in proper digestion.

If ever you decide that you need to clean your pet's teeth by yourself then you need to make sure that you do it right. Follow the steps below:

Step #1: Hold your pet's head. Make sure that you hold your schnoodle's face and slowly stick your finger in, and feel his gums. Your pet may initially resist it, but he'll eventually get used to it. If ever he doesn't cooperate at the moment then give it some time and don't force him.

Step #2: Start brushing! Once your dog got accustomed to it, you can then add toothpaste to your finger and rub it along your dog's teeth. After brushing it, make sure to open his mouth and check if his teeth and gums look healthy.

Step #3: Do a routine check. If ever you see any rotting teeth or if you notice that your dog has a bad breath, it is best that you immediately make an appointment with the doctor because it could be a sign of internal or digestive problems so that you can prevent it as early as possible.

How to Trim Your Dog's Nails

You want to make sure that you always check your dog's nails, and get him accustomed to your handling in order to make them feel at ease whenever you're clipping its nails. You need to trim your pet's nails at least twice or thrice a week using nail clippers that's suitable for your pet schnoodle.

The first thing to do is to push back the skin and make sure you can see the part of the nail you want to clip.

Make sure to watch out for the quick; a quick is the vein that runs down the center of the nail that can cause bleeding if it's accidentally cut. If ever you do trim it, don't panic, and always have a quick stop handy. Just apply the quick stop and press it down to stop the bleeding. Ensure that the dewclaws are also cut and trimmed to the appropriate size.

Reminders When Cleaning Your Dog's Ears

A schnoodle's ears aren't erect compared to other dogs which is why it's very important that you always keep them clean because flopped out ears doesn't have as much airflow compared to erect ears thus it's more prone to bacteria infestations.

- Should you need to clean out your pet's ears, you may ask the vet first to show you the correct way in doing it to avoid harming your pet.

- Whenever you're cleaning your pet's ear, make sure to check the hair around the ears and inside the ears to see if there are any signs of ticks and mite infestations. If ever there is, immediately remove them and dab with antiseptic solution.

Chapter Seven: Health and Wellness for Your Schnoodle

This chapter will cover some of the most common diseases that your pet schnoodle can experience in its lifetime. Knowledge about these diseases or hereditary illnesses can help you prevent and identify the onset of the disease. As a responsible keeper, it's essential for you to know about these problems including the possible causes, obvious symptoms, and possible treatments. We highly recommend that before you even acquire a schnoodle, your breeder or your local vet will give you a heads up as to what kind of problems you can encounter especially with designer breeds like the schnoodle. Proper husbandry, balanced diet, and tender love and care are the keys to a happy pup!

Common Illnesses of Schnoodle Breed

Below are some of the most common diseases that schnoodle breeds encounter. The causes of the illnesses are usually hereditary or due to genetic factors since they are designer breeds. Poodles and Schnauzer canines will one way or another pass on certain genes that can affect your dog's health, though sometimes it's just plainly coincidental. Find out more in this section.

Gastric Dilatation and Volvulus Syndrome

GDV is also known as Gastric Torsion. It's an illness wherein the dog's stomach or digestion dilates, twists, and rotates in the short axis. The common effects of GDV to the dog are pressure within its abdomen, damage to the heart, progressive stomach problems, and also slow process of perfusion. (Perfusion is the process wherein nutrients are delivered in the blood to the different tissues and arteries). If perfusion is insufficient it may be fatal or lead to cellular/organ damage.

Symptoms

- Anxious behavior

- Abdominal pain
- Excessive drooling
- Extreme Vomiting
- Stomach Distension
- Collapse
- Rapid Heartbeat (Tachycardia)
- Dyspnea (heavy breathing)
- Weak pulse
- Pale colored mucus membrane in the nose/mouth

Causes

Just like the Legg-Calvé-Perthes Disease, Gastric Dilatation and Volvulus Syndrome's exact causes are also unknown. There are various factors like the physical anatomy, improper husbandry, and also genetic/hereditary factors.

If your dog's relative has been diagnosed with gastric torsion, then there's a high probability that your dog may also suffer from it. However, it's not as much common to small to medium size dogs or designer breeds because large canines are usually the ones that are affected by this including German Shepherds, and Great Danes. However, it still occurs in puppies so better be observant and ensure that you're feeding them a balanced diet, and regularly takes them to the vet for a routine check – up.

Other possible causes of gastric torsion is ingestion of excessive food/water, delayed bowel movements/ constipation, and also too much activity right after eating. Usually dogs that already have a medical history of experiencing other forms of gastrointestinal problems are mostly likely to suffer from GDV but of course it doesn't apply to every dog.

Treatment

If you see your dog suffering from Gastric Dilatation and Volvulus Syndrome, he/she will definitely require immediate treatment and even hospitalization at the vet clinic especially if heart problems are also present. The process of treating is through gastric decompression, or orogastric intubation. Orogastric intubation is when a tube is inserted through the dog's mouth that reaches its stomach. Once the dog is stabilized, organs will be returned to their normal positions. Gastropexy may also be done in order to prevent recurrence of gastric torsion; this is when the stomach of the dog is permanently secured.

Retinal Degeneration

The retina, similar in human beings, is the tissue in the eye that is located in the inner surface, and mainly functions as the brain's camera. It transmits visual information or images to the brain via the rods and cones, enabling a person or in this case a dog to see things. The retina belongs to the dog's Central Nervous System, and it's also the only part that can be examined by veterinarians.

If your dog has retinal degeneration, it simply means that there is a decline or decrease in the retina's cellular functions making the dog visually impaired, and can eventually lead to complete blindness.

Symptoms

- Night blindness
- Light blindness
- Dilated pupils
- The pupil of the dog has abnormal reactions to light
- Cannot clearly see when there's a bright light
- There are cases where the dog only loses the central vision functions and still retain peripheral vision
- Cataract may also be seen since the retinal structure is quite abnormal

- It's also linked with obesity and liver problems
- Sudden and complete blindness because the dog acquired SARDS or Sudden Acquired Retinal Degeneration Syndrome.

Causes

- This disease is usually due to genetic factors, which is why it's quite common in designer breeds like the schnoodle.

- Hereditary degeneration which is characterized by the faulty formation of a group of cells in the retina that also gradually lost its function.

- Degenerative; it eventually leads to glaucoma which is the separation of the retina, and also due to scarring inflammation.

- Abnormal structure which mostly occurs during labor, or there's an abnormal development of the dog's retina as they grow older.

- Metabolic; there's a lack of certain enzymes in the dog's body or excess amounts of it.

- Cancer; if the dog is diagnosed with cancer, it can eventually spread to the brain and affect the eye's retina.

- Idiopathic (Unknown Cause)

- Deficiency of Vitamin A or E

- It can be caused by spread of infections to the eye from other body parts

- Toxic materials

- Negative reactions to drugs or a form of side – effect.

Treatment

Unfortunately, vets and researchers still don't have a cure for retinal degeneration. There's no medication available, and surgery will not entirely cure it as well. However, vets believe that the main cause of it is due to a wrong diet which is why the only prevention you can do is to ensure that your dog is provided with a balanced, and low – fat diet just like BARF meal in order to improve the condition, or prevent retinal degeneration.

Cloudiness of the Eye Lens

Cloudiness of the Eye Lens is most commonly known as cataracts in dogs. It's another very common illness that designer breeds like the schnoodle experience. It is when a certain cloud or blur is formed in the eye which blocks vision. It can vary from complete opacity to partial opacity. If the iris is directly clouded, it will then prevent light from passing to the retina, thereby causing impaired vision.

Usually cataracts are inherited from their parent breeds. Some of the purebred and designer breeds that are very prone to cataracts include the Mini Poodle, Mini Schnauzer, Boston Terriers, American Cocker Spaniel, Siberian Huskies, and Golden Retrievers.

Symptoms

Symptoms are usually related depending on the degree of the visual impairment. For instance, dogs who experiences only 30% of visual opacity may only display few symptoms, if not at all. Whereas dogs who are already experiencing 60% opacity can already suffer from visually impairment, or owners notice that they are having difficulty seeing things when there's only little light.

If ever your schnoodle has Diabetes Mellitus, chances are, they will get cataract one way or another. Along with visual impairment symptoms, you may also see signs like weight loss, frequent urination, and they are thirstier than usual.

Causes

Even if most cataract cases are inherited from their parent breeds, other risk factors are linked to the following:

- Diabetes mellitus
- Old age
- Electric shock
- Inflammation of the eye's *uvea* (*uveitis*)
- *Hypocalcemia* or the abnormal low levels of calcium in blood
- Radiation or toxic substances exposure

Treatment

If your vet says that your dog needed surgery, then by all means do so. This is because cataracts are a type of progressive disorder which means that if it's not immediately prevented or given medication, it can rapidly lead to blindness of not just one but both of your pet's eyes especially if your dog is also diagnosed with Diabetes Mellitus, then surgery is a must. However, vets usually don't recommend surgery if the dog has a non – genetic form of cataract.

The cataract surgery usually involves the so – called Phacoemulsification technique, and often uses an ultrasonic hand piece. The process involves the eye's lens being emulsified so that it is replaced with a balanced salt solution that could also prevent farsightedness. Aside from this, intraocular lens may also be surgically implanted. This technique/ surgical procedure cure cataracts in dogs 90% of the time.

Disintegration of Hip Joint

Another common illness is known as the hip joint disintegration or the Legg-Calvé-Perthes Disease. This is when the head of the dog's femur bone is being degenerated which can result to coxofemoral (hip joint disintergration) or inflammation in the joints also known as osteoarthritis.

Causes

The exact cause of the disease is not yet known but vets and researchers believe that it's more genetic/

hereditary, and usually occurs with small designer breed dogs that may have begun with the Manchester Terriers. This disease is usually detected around 5 to 8 months of age.

Symptoms

- Gradual lethargy
- Limping
- Pain when moving the hip joint
- Wasting of thigh muscles on the affected joints

Treatment

Vets usually recommend medications like pain killers and crate/bed rest. They also advise cold packing as it can help in preventing your dog from becoming lethargic.

If ever surgery is done, exercise of the femur bone head as well as their neck is required after the procedure or some form of physical therapy in order to rehabilitate the affected hip/joints/limbs.

Chapter Summary

This chapter will provide you with an overview of your newfound pet schnoodle! Take note of these things as they might come handy. Keeping a designer breed like schnoodle dogs are both fun and fulfilling. For newbie keepers, it might be quite a lot of work at first especially during the housebreaking and training, not to mention all the other things you need to do like preparing their meals every day, providing them with all their basic necessities, making sure that they are healthy, and really investing time in them through dog walks, playtime, and exercise. Doing all these things is all part of becoming a responsible dog keeper. It's going to be tough at first but in the long run, you'll realize that the love you give to your pet will be returned to you a hundred fold!

Biological Information

- **Height:** 25 to 38 cm (9.8 inches to 15 inches) for males; its female counterpart has a slightly smaller height to the shoulder.

- **Weight:** 14 to 24 pounds (5.4 to 11 kilogram) for males. Female schnoodles has a relatively lesser weight than its male counterparts.

-

- **Coat Type:** The schnoodle coat sports either a short or long coat that can also have a variety of soft or silky loose curly coat, a tight curl, or a straight coat.

- **Coat Colors:** Brown, Black, White, Gray, Silver, Sable, Apricot, Black & White, Black & Tan

-

- **Common Schnoodle Dog Names:** For males: Jax, Spike, Ziggy, Joey, Luke, Bo, Romeo, Sparky, Ollie, and Tyson; for females: Lulu, Shelby, Daisy, Cookie, Missy, Bonnie, Sasha, Pepper, Delilah and Molly.

- **Pros of Owning a Schnoodle:** Schnoodles are indoor pets, they are very friendly and easily trained, Schnoodles have an allergen – free coat and are also a non – shedders

- **Cons of Owning a Schnoodle:** Schnoodles are barkers, Schnoodle is not a purebred dog, and they are usually prone to various genetic illnesses from their parent breeds.

How to Select the Right Pup

Color Coding Technique

Step 1: Observe: Once the breeder has led you to the play pen where the puppies are, all you have to do is observe how the puppies play with one another. You can lean over them and let them sniff your finger, and see how they'll react. If the puppies are interactive to you, that's a good sign of how social and friendly they are.

Step 2: Start interacting with the pups: You might want to proceed inside the play pen and be with the puppies. You can also ask the breeder to put in another puppy that is of a different breed (if they have any) so that you can see how the schnoodles will react and welcome another kind.

Step 3: Start interacting with the pups one – on – one: Put them through your own "personal test" to see which one best suits you or perhaps best connect with you

Attention Seeker Method: What you can do is to walk around the play pen and see which dogs follow you, and which ones aren't interested. This will help you see how much these puppies want your attention.

Lie on the floor Technique: The next thing you can do is to make the puppy lie on its back and see whether he/she tends to bite you or not. This will determine if the dog is someone who can easily be trained or not.

The Cuddle Factor Method: This is where you can see if the puppy is into you, and someone whom you feel connected to. You just simply have to cuddle the puppy and hold them in your hands, and lean them over your chest or shoulder just like a baby then see how he/she will react.

Housing and Crate Training

Benefits of Using Crates for Pups and Dogs

- Environmental Management
- Errorless Housetraining for puppies
- Crates provide housetraining for newly adopted dogs

Types of Crates

- Plastic Crates
- Wire Crates
- Soft – Sided Crates

- Fashion Crates
- Heavy Duty Crates
- Exercise Pens

Crate Tip:

- The wire crate will function as an inclusion crate wherein the dog is housed but it's still in close proximity with its owners.

- The plastic crate will function as the quiet crate which will provide your pet with some quiet time alone.

Size of the Crate

- Wire crates usually come with a small divider so that once your pet starts growing, you can easily adjust and enlarge the cage so that you don't need to keep buying.

- For your plastic crate you may need to buy a crate big enough to accommodate your schnoodle's growth.

Crate Training

- **Habituation:** Your goal here is to let your dog view the crate as a safe place that's also a pleasant and comfortable environment.

- **Timing:** Ideally, you want to crate train them once they've already worn out or tired after playing around all day because that will initiate them to settle down inside their crate and take some rest after a long day.

Tips in Crate Training Your Pet

- Tip #1: Use your voice and praise your dog.
- Tip #2: Tie the back door of the crate
- Tip #3: Keep a bowl of treats and some toys in the crate.
- Tip #4: Avoid predictable crate training times.
- Tip #5: Never let your dog make a habit of demanding to be let up in the crate.

Supplies for Your Schnoodle

Dog Essentials:

- Food and Water
- Food/Water Bowls

- Dog Bed
- Collar and ID
- Lead
- Brush
- Toys
- Dog Shampoo/ Soap

Optional Items:

- Harness
- Clicker
- Training Treats
- Deodorizer Spray
- Fur and Nail Clippers
- Child Gates

Feeding Your Schnoodle

The BARF Diet Ingredients

Meat:

- Raw chicken with bones (small/ bite – sized/ large; depending on the age/size of your dog)
- Frozen Minced Turkey
- Frozen Minced Chicken
- Egg (1)

- Beef chunks

Veggies/ Fruits

- Carrots (at least 1)
- Apples (1 to 2 apples sliced)
- Broccoli (just a handful of chooped broccolis)

Feeding Schedule:

- **3 to 4 months:** 2 meals per day (same food)
- **7 to 9 months:** 1 meal a day
- **8 to 10 months onwards:** 1 meal a day (you can gradually start switching to adult dog foods)

Grooming Tips for Your Schnoodle

- Get rid of the clumps of hair
- Add a few drops of conditioner in the water and spray it to your dog's coat.
- Use the comb to untangle the mats and knots if there's any and loosen the dead hair.
- Flatten the coat

Health and Wellness

Common Illnesses of Schnoodle Breed

- Gastric Dilatation and Volvulus Syndrome
- Retinal Degeneration
- Cloudiness of the Eye Lens
- Disintegration of Hip Joint

Glossary of Dog Terms

Abundism – Referring to a pup that has markings more prolific than is normal.

Acariasis – A type of mite infection.

ACF – Australian Pup Federation

Affix – A puptery name that follows the pup's registered name; puptery owner, not the breeder of the pup.

Agouti – A type of natural coloring pattern in which individual hairs have bands of light and dark coloring.

Ailurophile – A person who loves pups.

Albino – A type of genetic mutation which results in little to no pigmentation, in the eyes, skin, and coat.

Allbreed – Referring to a show that accepts all breeds or a judge who is qualified to judge all breeds.

Alley Pup – A non-pedigreed pup.

Alter – A desexed pup; a male pup that has been neutered or a female that has been spayed.

Amino Acid – The building blocks of protein; there are 22 types for pups, 11 of which can be synthesized and 11 which must come from the diet (see essential amino acid).

Anestrus – The period between estrus cycles in a female pup.

Any Other Variety (AOV) – A registered pup that doesn't conform to the breed standard.

ASH – American Shorthair, a breed of pup.

Back Cross – A type of breeding in which the offspring is mated back to the parent.

Balance – Referring to the pup's structure; proportional in accordance with the breed standard.

Barring – Describing the tabby's striped markings.

Base Color – The color of the coat.

Bicolor – A pup with patched color and white.

Blaze – A white coloring on the face, usually in the shape of an inverted V.

Bloodline – The pedigree of the pup.

Brindle – A type of coloring, a brownish or tawny coat with streaks of another color.

Castration – The surgical removal of a male pup's testicles.

Pup Show – An event where pups are shown and judged.

Puptery – A registered pup breeder; also, a place where pups may be boarded.

CFA – The Pup Fanciers Association.

Cobby – A compact body type.

Colony – A group of pups living wild outside.

Color Point – A type of coat pattern that is controlled by color point alleles; pigmentation on the tail, legs, face, and ears with an ivory or white coat.

Colostrum – The first milk produced by a lactating female; contains vital nutrients and antibodies.

Conformation – The degree to which a pedigreed pup adheres to the breed standard.

Cross Breed – The offspring produced by mating two distinct breeds.

Dam – The female parent.

Declawing – The surgical removal of the pup's claw and first toe joint.

Developed Breed – A breed that was developed through selective breeding and crossing with established breeds.

Down Hairs – The short, fine hairs closest to the body which keep the pup warm.

DSH – Domestic Shorthair.

Estrus – The reproductive cycle in female pups during which she becomes fertile and receptive to mating.

Fading Pup Syndrome – Pups that die within the first two weeks after birth; the cause is generally unknown.

Feral – A wild, untamed pup of domestic descent.

Gestation – Pregnancy; the period during which the fetuses develop in the female's uterus.

Guard Hairs – Coarse, outer hairs on the coat.

Harlequin – A type of coloring in which there are van markings of any color with the addition of small patches of the same color on the legs and body.

Inbreeding – The breeding of related pups within a closed group or breed.

Kibble – Another name for dry pup food.

Lilac – A type of coat color that is pale pinkish-gray.

Line – The pedigree of ancestors; family tree.

Litter – The name given to a group of pups born at the same time from a single female.

Mask – A type of coloring seen on the face in some breeds.

Matts – Knots or tangles in the pup's fur.

Mittens – White markings on the feet of a pup.

Moggie – Another name for a mixed breed pup.

Mutation – A change in the DNA of a cell.

Muzzle – The nose and jaws of an animal.

Natural Breed – A breed that developed without selective breeding or the assistance of humans.

Neutering – Desexing a male pup.

Open Show – A show in which spectators are allowed to view the judging.

Pads – The thick skin on the bottom of the feet.

Particolor – A type of coloration in which there are markings of two or more distinct colors.

Patched – A type of coloration in which there is any solid color, tabby, or tortoiseshell color plus white.

Pedigree – A purebred pup; the pup's papers showing its family history.

Pet Quality – A pup that is not deemed of high enough standard to be shown or bred.

Piebald – A pup with white patches of fur.

Points – Also color points; markings of contrasting color on the face, ears, legs, and tail.

Pricked – Referring to ears that sit upright.

Purebred – A pedigreed pup.

Queen – An intact female pup.

Roman Nose – A type of nose shape with a bump or arch.

Scruff – The loose skin on the back of a pup's neck.

Selective Breeding – A method of modifying or improving a breed by choosing pups with desirable traits.

Senior – A pup that is more than 5 but less than 7 years old.

Sire – The male parent of a pup.

Solid – Also self; a pup with a single coat color.

Spay – Desexing a female pup.

Stud – An intact male pup.

Tabby – A type of coat pattern consisting of a contrasting color over a ground color.

Tom Pup – An intact male pup.

Tortoiseshell – A type of coat pattern consisting of a mosaic of red or cream and another base color.

Tri-Color – A type of coat pattern consisting of three distinct colors in the coat.

Tuxedo – A black and white pup.

Unaltered – A pup that has not been desexed.

Photo Credits

Page 1 Photo by user Mathew via Flickr.com,

https://www.flickr.com/photos/damnthetorpedoes/43859855
49/

Page 5 Photo by user Steve Rhode via Flickr.com,

https://www.flickr.com/photos/steverhode/3080176663/

Page 14 Photo by user Mathew via Flickr.com,

https://www.flickr.com/photos/damnthetorpedoes/42109190
09/

Page 22 Photo by user Mathew via Flickr.com,

https://www.flickr.com/photos/damnthetorpedoes/41648493
02/

Page 39 Photo by user grfx Playground via Flickr.com,

https://www.flickr.com/photos/thehillside/8127393037/in/ph
otostream/

Page 51 Photo by user grfx Playground via Flickr.com,

https://www.flickr.com/photos/thehillside/8289313008/

Page 59 Photo by user Scott Anderson via Flickr.com,

https://www.flickr.com/photos/cardscott/4091468362/

Page 72 Photo by user grfx Playground via Flickr.com,

https://www.flickr.com/photos/thehillside/13643350043/

Page 84 Photo by user via Flickr.com,

https://www.flickr.com/photos/thehillside/8127384419/in/ph
otolist

References

"Schnoodle" – PetGuide.com

http://www.petguide.com/breeds/dog/schnoodle/

"Schnoodle" – TheHappyPuppySite.com

https://thehappypuppysite.com/schnoodle/

"Schnoodle" – DogZone.com

http://www.dogzone.com/crossbreeds/schnoodle/

"The Pros and Cons of Schnoodles" - Written By Shailynn Krow via Mom.me

http://animals.mom.me/the-pros-and-cons-of-schnoodles-12542090.html

"Schnoodle: The Schnauzer Poodle Mix" - TotallyDogTraining.com

http://totallydogtraining.com/schnoodle/

"Choosing A Puppy" – APDT.co.uk

http://www.apdt.co.uk/dog-owners/choosing-a-puppy

"8 Must Have Puppy Products for Your Pet" – CesarsWay.com

https://www.cesarsway.com/dog-care/puppy/8-must-have-puppy-products-for-you

"Checklist of Dog Supplies for Your New Fur Kind" – Nylabone.com

https://www.nylabone.com/dog101/checklist-of-dog-supplies-for-your-new-fur-kid

"Raw Dog Food Dietary Concerns: Benefits and Risks" - WebMD.com

https://pets.webmd.com/dogs/guide/raw-dog-food-dietary-concerns-benefits-and-risks

"Raw and Natural Feeding Advice" - NaturesMenu.co.uk

https://www.naturesmenu.co.uk/advice-centre

"How to Care for a Schnoodle Dog" - Cuteness.com

https://www.cuteness.com/article/care-schnoodle-dog

"How to Groom a Schnoodle Dog" – Cuteness.com

https://www.cuteness.com/article/groom-schnoodle-dog

"Common Dog Diseases & Dangers" - Petmed.net.au

http://www.petmed.net.au/dog-breeds/schnoodle/

www.ingramcontent.com/pod-product-compliance
Lightning Source LLC
Chambersburg PA
CBHW062004040426
42447CB00010B/1902